EXPLORING
IRISH MUSIC
AND
DANCE

DIANNA BOULLIER

Born in Holywood, County Down, Dianna inherited her love of music from her grandfather who played flute and concertina. After experimenting with various instruments she eventually took up the fiddle in her early twenties. She has spent many years playing and meeting with musicians in sessions and at music festivals all over Ireland. She has played on television and radio on many occasions, along with her husband Nigel on banjo, and has played at gigs in Scotland, England, Toronto and Amsterdam. She teaches fiddle workshops at folk festivals and travels around Northern Ireland bringing traditional music to schoolchildren as part of the Arts Council/Department of Education's Jigtime programme. Dianna lives in Bangor, County Down, with Nigel and their two children Jack and Patrick, and passes on her knowledge of Irish music by giving fiddle lessons.

Dianna with sons Jack and Patrick,
and husband Nigel

EXPLORING
ıRish music
AND dance

Dianna Boullier

Illustrated by Julian Friers

THE O'BRIEN PRESS
DUBLIN
IRISH AMERICAN BOOK COMPANY (IABC)
BOULDER, COLORADO

First published 1998 by The O'Brien Press Ltd.,
20 Victoria Road, Rathgar, Dublin 6, Ireland.
Tel. +353 1 4923333 Fax. +353 1 4922777
e-mail: books@obrien.ie   http://www.obrien.ie

Published in the US and Canada by the
Irish American Book Company (IABC)
6309 Monarch Park Place, Niwot, Colorado, 80503
Telephone (303) 530-1352, (800) 452-7115
Fax (303) 530-4488, (800) 401-9705

ISBN: 0-86278-558-8

British Library Cataloguing-in-publication Data
Boullier, Dianna
Exploring Irish music and dance
1. Music – Ireland 2. Music – Ireland – History and criticism
3. Dance – Ireland 4. Dance – Ireland – History
5. Irish – Music 6. Irish – Songs and music
I. Title
781.6'09415

1 2 3 4 5 6 7 8 9 10
97 98 99 00 01 02 03 04 05

With assistance from the Arts Council of
Northern Ireland for research.
The O'Brien Press receives
assistance from

The Arts Council
An Chomhairle Ealaíon

Typesetting, layout, design: The O'Brien Press Ltd.
Cover illustration: Anne Farrall
Back cover photograph: John Doherty with 'daughter of the house', McIntyre's pub,
Ballyshannon, County Donegal, taken by Eamonn O'Doherty
Cover separations: Lithoset Ltd., Dublin
Printing: MPG Books Ltd.

The counties of Ireland

ACKNOWLEDGEMENTS

Thanks to everyone who helped with this book, especially Chrissie Wylde, Liam Logan, Julian Friers, Bernard Astocks, Janet Harbison and Íde ní Laoghaire for all their time and effort. Thanks also to Len Graham, Derek Bell, Ciaran Carson, Nigel Boullier, John Hughes, Tom McGonigle, Robbie Hannan, Gerry O'Connor, Geordie McAdam, Caroline Judge, Bernie Graham, Fintan Vallely, Emily Skillen, Mary Fox, Lee McKillen, Marie Boullier, Linda McMullin, Graeme Kirkham, Jane at Claddagh Records, Lenny and Rachel at RTÉ, Nicholas Carolan and Harry Bradshaw at the Traditional Music Archive and Arts Council of Northern Ireland.

THE PHOTOGRAPHS

CONTENTS

THE TUNES

Introduction

During the sixties, owing largely to the efforts of Seán Ó Riada, Paddy Moloney, The Dubliners, Seán O'Boyle, Brendan Breathnach and many others, our vast heritage of folk music underwent a considerable revival, a revival which still goes on today! Indeed, this fine new book might well be considered part of that revival. The result of it was that some people began to take our music seriously as a noble music which should be listened to with deep attention. Strange to say many musicians and members of the public still believe that the only decent place to play or hear Irish music is, half drunk, in some overcrowded pub, probably poisoning one's spine, brain and liver with overindulgence in alcohol! I take my hat off to Dr Paddy Moloney, the founder and boss of my band The Chieftains: for nearly 35 years, he has taken our beautiful music out of the pubs and into the best concert halls in the world where it can be listened to with devoted attention without the accompaniment of clinking glasses, conversation and smoke!

How nice to welcome and introduce this excellent book for younger people who should not yet be frequenting the pubs! Little, so far, has been written to explain our music to them, and the need is great. The introduction to this book makes it very clear that our music is of much interest; that it is for our enjoyment and not just our education! Young people should learn to read music, but it is equally important that they also learn by ear and they should develop both abilities as far as possible.

While dance teachers and music teachers will have to explain in more detail the different dance rhythms, and the fact that Irish music (in addition to dance music) consists of a wealth of harp music; a body of airs; unaccompanied, beautifully ornamented sean-nós vocal music and even religious music in monasteries and university libraries (some of this only recently discovered by Mícheál Ó Súilleabháin and Nóirín Ní Riain), this book explains the naming of tunes, the 'bones' and form of tunes, it highlights regional styles and contains a note about every instrument one is likely to find among people playing Irish music.

A charming feature of this book is the inclusion of several legends and fairy tales, the most attractive and entrancing being 'The Fairy Dance', 'The Piper and the Pooka'. The book finishes with short biographies of prominent local musicians and some musicians of national and international importance.

The book should prove beneficial, explanatory and enjoyable not only for the young people for whom it is especially intended, but also for mature grown-ups and I wish it every possible success all over the world where our great treasury of folk music is loved and appreciated.

Derek Bell
Bangor, Co Down

Foreword

Since the dawn of time people have enjoyed making and listening to music.

Every country in the world has its own musical history and each has its own special array of blown, plucked and struck instruments. Ireland is no exception. We are fortunate to have a very rich tradition of instrumental music.

Indian musicians

This book describes traditional music, the instruments commonly used and the types of tunes you are likely to hear. An important thing to remember is that traditional music is an enjoyable pastime. If there is no pleasure in music-making eventually there is no music. As the fiddle player Kevin Burke says in the sleeve notes to his 1978 recording 'If the Cap Fits':

Japanese musicians

Something I'll always remember about the Irish musicians I met when I was a child, was that there was always an element of fun, pure fun, in their playing and their music. Sometimes this gave way to a plaintive, wistful mood, but the fun was never far away.

The world of traditional music is hugely interesting and enjoyable.

And here it is on your doorstep ...

Irish musicians from the early twentieth century

CHAPTER ONE

Traditional Music

Traditional music has been played for centuries all over Ireland. It has been handed down from father to son, from mother to daughter, from neighbour to neighbour; and it still is, for Irish music is a living tradition. Music played today is not exactly the same as that played in the eighteenth and nineteenth centuries. It has changed in its journey through time, from person to person, from area to area. New rhythms have been explored, others forgotten; new tunes have been composed and many others lost. But today's music is a continuation of the ancient music of Ireland.

THE ORAL TRADITION

Irish music belongs to an oral tradition. Tunes are learned by listening, watching and trying to imitate other players. This is called 'playing by ear'. Only in the past two hundred years have a great many of the jigs, reels and hornpipes been written down, and only recently have traditional musicians been able to read them. A great many musicians still play only by ear and cannot read music. Many say that a tune

Donegal fiddler Johnny Doherty

learned by the 'notes' (that is, from written music), is more easily forgotten than one learned from listening to another player. Also, if you learn a tune by ear you then associate it with the person you heard playing it or the place where you happened to be when you first heard it; so the tune is alive in your mind and not just dead black dots on a white page.

It can be very useful, however, to have the ability to read music. If you hear a tune, like it and decide to learn it, you may not be able to remember it, so, reading the tune from a music book will jolt your memory. Sometimes difficult phrases can be grasped more easily by reading from music.

CÉILÍ HOUSES

In days gone by, long before television, video and CDs, people entertained themselves with music, dancing and singing. They would gather round the kitchen fire and exchange tunes, songs and stories. Places where these gatherings were held were called céilí houses and musicians were always welcome. Johnny Doherty, a well-known fiddler in Donegal, used to travel all round the county playing at dances, parties, country fairs and the like. Sometimes he didn't bring his own fiddle with him, for he knew all the houses where there was a fiddle hanging on the wall just waiting to be played. It was to these céilí houses that he travelled, where he'd always have a great welcome.

Meeting and playing together is important to traditional musicians but nowadays the gathering is less likely to be a farmhouse kitchen and more often a hotel or lounge bar. These gatherings are known as 'sessions'.

Last Night's Fun

LOCAL STYLES

A fiddler or flute player from one area might play a tune in one way while a player in another area, perhaps only a few miles away, might play the same tune in a different way, in a different style. Sometimes the tune has a different name as well.

A quadrille tune played in County Down is called 'Who'll be King but Charlie?' A different version is played in Donegal: 'Tá do Mhargadh Déanta' and also has words. 'Behind the Bush in the Garden', a jig played by New York fiddler Andy McGann, is the same tune.

Who'll be King but Charlie?

Nowadays it is much easier to hear players from different areas. Look at all the CDs available: you can hear musicians from every corner of Ireland as well as America, Canada and elsewhere. Now we have cars that can take us twenty or

Behind the Bush in the Garden

thirty miles down the road, and planes that can take us hundreds of miles, to hear someone play. Before all these modern inventions people had to be content with hearing fiddlers and pipers in their own neighbourhood, or perhaps a travelling fiddle teacher. The result was that people usually played in the style of the area where they lived. This is not the case today. Anyone learning an instrument can copy a player or several players that they admire. So, instead of having a recognisable local style, players tend to develop their own individual style of playing.

CHAPTER TWO

Dancing

Now o'er the floor in wanton pairs
They foot it to the fiddle
The maidens muster a' their airs
The young men skip an' striddle

from 'The Country Dance' by Samuel Thompson,
the Bard of Carngranny, *c.*1793

People have danced in Ireland since pre-Christian times. Celtic druids worshipped the sun and trees with rituals that involved dancing in a circle. This continued and developed into the Christian era. Unfortunately there are no written records of this development. Dances only began to be written down with the appearance of dancing masters in the eighteenth century. Dancing Masters travelled around the country, sometimes accompanied by a fiddler or piper, teaching dances in return for money. They are thought to be responsible for creating steps which are still danced today. They based these steps on European dances, especially the French Cotillion and the Quadrilles.

The Cotillion was danced by four couples facing the centre in a square formation. The dance had several separate parts or figures. The Quadrilles were a similar dance and became very popular in Ireland around 1820. The name 'Quadrilles' is thought to be derived from an Italian word, 'Quadriglia', meaning a troop of horsemen who formed a square when taking part in a tournament. As in the Cotillion, the Quadrilles were and still are danced by four couples facing each other in a square. This formation is called a 'set'. Each traditional set dance is arranged into a number of separate dances called figures. In the set of Quadrilles

there are six figures. Each figure varies in length, usually three or four minutes. Modern set dancing is a continuation of the Quadrilles.

Styles of dancing and figures vary throughout the country, showing that over a period of time they evolved to suit different communities. Dancing is a very social activity. Dancing at crossroads, and house and village dances were popular all over Ireland until the 1950s. They provided an enjoyable distraction from the hardships of everyday life. Today more and more people are enjoying set dancing and there are lots of different dances, for example, 'Cavan Reel

Set dancing

Set', 'Clare Lancers', 'Paris Set', 'Ballyvourney Jig Set', 'Waltz Cotillion', 'Kenmare Polka Set'.

The music for set dancing can be played by an accordion or fiddle player, or more usually these days by a group of musicians.

SOLO DANCING

Ireland has a long tradition of solo dancing. The hornpipe is a popular solo dance. It is always performed in hard shoes and the dancer can beat out complex rhythms on the floor to complement the music. Double and slip jigs can be danced solo, also in hard shoes so that the dancer can display his or her skill and agility. Earlier this century it was common in rural Ireland for the door of the house to be taken off its hinges and placed on the floor for a dancer, so that the onlookers could appreciate the intricate footwork. Another tradition, in houses where dances took place, was the burial of a horse's skull under the floor. This was supposed to improve the sound of the dancer's feet on the ground.

Some solo dances have specific patterns of steps and are only danced to one tune. These are known as set dances, 'set' in this case meaning that the steps are the same every time the dance is performed. This is different to set dancing where the set is the square formation of four couples. 'The Three Sea Captains', 'The Blackbird' and 'Rodney's Glory' are set dances. In County Limerick set dances were known as table dances because the dancer often jumped on to the kitchen table to dance. Like dancing on the door, the table helped to display the skilful footwork of the dancer.

CÉILÍ DANCING

Traditional music is also played for céilí dancing. Dances such as 'The Walls of Limerick', 'The Waves of Tory' and 'The Siege of Ennis' were created at the turn of the century and became very popular in the 1920s and 1930s. Céilí dances are performed in 'lines' and any number of couples can join in. The music is played by a céilí band. These bands have drums and a piano and hence a very distinctive sound.

The Fairy Dance

In Irish folklore there are lots and lots of stories about fairies. Many of these involve music and dance, fairies often giving the gift of music to mortals in return for something. In this story a young girl has a taste of fairy life.

November is the month of spirits and enchantment. One evening at the beginning of November, Eileen, the prettiest girl in the village, was going to the well for water. Suddenly her foot slipped and she fell. But when she got up and looked around it seemed as if she was in a different place, as if under a spell. In the distance she saw a crowd of people gathered around a bonfire.

Slowly she walked towards them as if some invisible power was drawing her. Soon she found herself among the crowd. She was very frightened, as they all stared strangely at her. But when she tried to run away she couldn't move. A handsome boy with long blonde hair then came up and asked her if she would dance with him.

'How can I dance with you,' asked Eileen, 'when there is no music?'

The boy lifted his hand and made some sort of sign. Suddenly the air was filled with beautiful music, the mellow sounds of flute and fiddle. The yellow-haired boy took Eileen's arm and they began to dance. They danced and danced. They danced all night long. Eileen felt as though she was floating on a cloud. She was not tired. She forgot everything but the music, the dance and her handsome partner.

At last the music stopped and the dance ended. The boy thanked Eileen and invited her to join them all for some supper. She saw an opening in the ground with a flight of dark steps leading down, down. The young man took Eileen's hand and led her down the steps to a huge banqueting hall brightly lit with beautiful gold and silver candles. A great table was spread with good things to eat. There were golden goblets of wine for them to drink. Everyone sat down and began the feast. The handsome boy passed a goblet of wine to Eileen and she held the golden cup to her lips. Just then a man passed behind her and whispered,

'Eat no food and drink no wine, or you'll never see your home again.'

The Enchanted Lady

Eileen put the golden goblet on to the table and refused to drink. Everybody in the banqueting hall was quiet and stared angrily at her. A fierce, dark-haired man suddenly jumped up and shouted,

'Whoever comes to us must drink with us!'

He grabbed her arm and pushed the wine towards her lips. Poor Eileen almost died of fright! Just at that moment a red-haired man stood up. He gave a loud yell, took Eileen by the hand and led her up and out of the underground hall.

'You are safe this time,' he said, handing her a branch of ground ivy. 'Take this creeping herb. Hold it close until you reach home and no one will harm you.'

Eileen ran away into the darkness. She was very frightened. Her heart was thumping and she could hear footsteps following her. Clasping the ground ivy up to her chin she glanced back, but she couldn't see anyone. Tired and out of breath she at last reached home. She locked the door behind her and rested by the fire until she got her breath back. Later she climbed up to bed. She was lying in the darkness, almost asleep, when loud shouting began outside.

'We had power over you. Now it is gone through the magic herb, but when you dance again to the music on the hill, you will stay with us forever!'

Eileen never did dance again to the fairy music on the hill, for she kept a piece of the magic ivy with her always. But neither did she ever forget the music of the fiddle and flute that night, nor the beautiful yellow-haired fairy who danced with her.

CHAPTER THREE

The Music

Written music is simply a way of representing on paper what is played on an instrument. It is a kind of language and, as with any language, you don't have to be able to read or write to speak the language or, in the case of music, to play it. Traditional music is learned by listening, watching and playing. It is not necessary to be able to read music to play traditional music.

FLESH AND BONES

When a tune is written down, only the basic melody is recorded. This is called the bones of a tune. The flesh or ornamentation is added by the individual musician when the tune is played. Each musician will add his or her own ornamentation. Although no two musicians will play a tune exactly the same way, they are able to play the tune together because the bones of the tune remain the same. When the basic melody alters then this becomes a different version of the tune. Two different versions of the same tune cannot be played at the same time. Look at the example in the last chapter; the quadrille tune from County Down, 'Who'll be King but Charlie?'. This tune, and 'Behind the Bush in the Garden', are two versions of one tune but they could not be played at the same time.

Most tunes have two parts. The 'A' music or first eight bars is known as 'the tune' and is played twice, making sixteen bars. The 'B' music, known as 'the turn', is then played twice, making another sixteen bars. (In 'Casey the Whistler', below, the first four bars are repeated to make eight, then all repeated again.)

Casey the Whistler

This makes up the whole tune of thirty-two bars and may be played two, three or as many times as the musician wants. Then another tune can be joined on and played afterwards. This means that groups of musicians playing together in a session can change or finish tunes at the same time. Before playing the musicians will decide how many times to play each tune. If two or three tunes are played together they are usually the same type of tune – all double jigs, all polkas, all reels etc. Occasionally different types of tunes may be played together. For example, a strathspey can be followed by a reel.

The Kid on the Mountain

Sometimes tunes have more than two parts. 'The Kid on the Mountain' is a four-part slip jig.

THE NAMES OF TUNES

It is always easier to remember a tune if it has a name. Tunes are given names for lots of different reasons and most of them have absolutely nothing to do with the melody. Sometimes they are named after a particular musician. For example, 'Jimmy Ward's Jig' is named after a banjo player from County Clare; 'O'Keeffe's Slide' is named after fiddle master Pádraig O'Keeffe of County Kerry.

Other tunes are named after the composer of the tune: 'Paddy Fahy's Reel' is by Paddy Fahy, a fiddle player from County Galway; 'Paddy Mills' Delight' is a tune composed by fiddler Paddy Mills of County Mayo.

Tune titles can be linked with an event in history, as in 'Napoleon Crossing the Rhine', a hornpipe, or 'Bonaparte's Retreat', a set dance. This does not mean that these tunes were composed at that time.

Local placenames are often mentioned in tune titles: 'Rathfriland Lasses', 'Galway Hornpipe', 'Humours of Tulla', 'Mullingar Races', 'Pretty Girls of Mayo', 'Lads of Laois', 'Long Hills of Mourne', and so on. In fact, tunes can be

Rainy Day

named after anything at all, as the following list shows: 'Lark in the Morning', 'New Policeman', 'Rainy Day', 'Christmas Eve', 'Devenney's Goat', 'Bag of Spuds', 'When Sick is it Tea You Want?', 'Happy to Meet Sorry to Part', 'The Cat that Ate the Candle', 'Tear the Calico', 'I Have no Money'.

Sometimes tunes can have more than one title. 'The Flowing Bowl' is a common reel played in every county in Ireland. It is also

Bag of Spuds

known as 'The Piper's Despair'. Liz Carroll, a fiddler from Chicago, calls it 'Curly Mike'. Another reel, 'The Perthshire Hunt', was composed around 1780 by a Miss Stirling of Ardoch in Scotland. It is better known in Ireland as 'The Boyne Hunt', but it is also known by forty other names.

The Cat that Ate the Candle

Johnny Doherty, a great Donegal fiddle player, called it 'The Sailor's Trip to Liverpool'.

Occasionally titles fit the melody of the tune, e.g. 'Old Molly Doodle Will you not Come Out', 'Shoe the Donkey', 'Merrily Kiss the Quaker's Wife'. Tunes like these would have been lilted at a dance if there was no musician to play or if no one owned a musical instrument. This was very often the case in poor, rural communities. Lilting is also known as diddling, mouth music or gob music. The tune is 'sung' by the lilter using words such as 'Rum diddly um dee skiddery idle um dee' etc. Styles vary from lilter to lilter. Johnny Loughran of Pomeroy, County Tyrone, was a wonderful lilter and used 'words' such as 'Quiddly quidden clod' when he lilted a tune. Pat Kilduff, another great lilter, can be heard on 'The Chieftains 3', recorded in 1971 by Claddagh Records. In fact Irish music is sometimes called Diddly Dee Music (usually by people who don't like it, or don't understand it). If one is lilting for a long time, the mouth becomes very tired, so to rest the muscles (different muscles are used for lilting

than those used for singing), nonsense words are sung to the
tune. 'The Hen's Schottische' has these words:

> *Maggie picking on the shore*
> *Gathering winkles off Culmore*
> *Lifts her leg and lets a roar*
> *What the Devil ails you!*

In a few cases a tune title has a whole story behind it, like this
one, 'The Fairies' Hornpipe'.

The Fairies' Hornpipe

The Fairies' Hornpipe

Joe, a piper, was out very late one night, playing at a dance.
On his way home he decided to take a short cut through the
fields instead of going the long way home by the road. His
box for the set of pipes was very heavy and he was tired after
playing at the dance. Off he set through the fields, but it
seemed to be taking him ages and ages to get home. Anyway,

eventually he noticed that he kept coming back to the same gap in the hedge. He had heard that the fairies can make you go round and round in circles, in a kind of enchantment. They keep you walking all night until you are absolutely exhausted.

'They must find it very funny to watch or something,' thought Joe to himself. Now, fortunately Joe knew how to break this spell. He took off his jacket, turned it inside out and put it back on, still inside out. Sure enough, when he looked down the hill he could see his mother's cottage only two fields away.

Down the first sloping field he went. As he approached the bottom of the hill he thought he could hear music. He hid himself quietly under a hawthorn bush and peeped out. Dawn was breaking and there was just enough light for him to see a little group of fairies dancing to the music of a fairy piper sitting on a grassy hillock. He sat under the bush, listening and enjoying the music, enjoying it so much that it soothed him to sleep. When he awoke the sun was high in the sky. The fairies were gone. So Joe hurried home to find his mother busy cooking breakfast.

'Joe,' she said, 'You're back at last. Whatever kept you out 'til this hour of the morning?' And he told her the whole story: getting lost, turning his jacket the wrong way out and hearing the fairy music.

'You expect me to believe that!' laughed his mother, thinking that he had been at some party or other all night.

'Well,' said Joe, 'isn't my jacket turned inside out!' Still she didn't believe him.

Suddenly Joe opened his box and lifted out the set of pipes. He strapped them on. 'Before I fell asleep under the hawthorn bush the fairy piper was playing this tune.' Joe began to play. His mother had never heard the tune before, and neither had anyone else that Joe played it for. So his mother had to believe his strange story. And to this day the tune is known as 'The Fairies' Hornpipe'.

WHO COMPOSES THE TUNES?

There are thousands and thousands of traditional dance tunes. People often wonder who made them all up. The truth is no one knows. Musicians are composing tunes all the time. Perhaps the composer of a tune plays it a few times. Someone hears it and learns it, then someone else, then someone else and so on. This is the way traditional music works. Tunes are passed from person to person. The composer of the tune may or may not be remembered; and the tune will change in its journey from person to person, from place to place, from yesterday to tomorrow.

Some composers of tunes, however, are remembered, as we have seen through the naming of tunes. But, more usually the composer is known these days because the tune has been recorded on tape or CD or else has been published in a music book.

Liz Carroll of Chicago has composed many fine tunes, some of which you can hear on her fiddle recordings. Most of her tunes are quite complicated and difficult to play.

Tony Sullivan, a banjo player from Manchester, also composes many tunes which he publishes in music tutors. His best known tunes, 'The Arkle Mountain' and 'The Exile from Erin' (reels), are often heard in music sessions throughout the country.

Liz Carroll

Ed Reavy, a fiddle player from County Cavan and a very well-known composer of traditional tunes, spent most of his life in Philadelphia, USA. He published 79 tunes in a book called *Where the River Shannon Rises* and every traditional player would know a few of his tunes.

Susie and Tony Sullivan

TYPES OF TUNE

In traditional Irish music there are many different rhythms and dances. The most commonly played dance tunes are jigs, reels and hornpipes. The beat or rhythm is the feature that distinguishes one type of tune from another. To dance a jig the musician must play a jig; or if the dance is a hornpipe he or she must play a hornpipe, not a polka or a waltz. Each type of tune is in a specific rhythm and goes hand in hand with the dance.

The Stack of Barley

Jigs

The jig is a very old dance and there are three types: double jig, slip or hop jig and single jig or slide.

SINGLE JIG

The Brosna Slide

Double jigs are heard most frequently and most of the ones played today were composed by fiddlers and pipers in the eighteenth and nineteenth centuries. Others were made up from old marches and songs and some were borrowed from English traditional music. The very first Irish Jig to be written down was composed by a harper from County Sligo, Thomas Connellan. It is included in a book called *Neale's Celebrated Irish Tunes*, published in 1726.

DOUBLE JIG

The Boys of Our Town

SLIP JIG

Comb Your Hair and Curl It

Reels

Most musicians today enjoy playing reels and know more reels than any other type of tune. Reels are mentioned in music collections printed at the end of the eighteenth century and are thought to have come to Ireland from Scotland.

'Bonnie Kate', 'The Boyne Hunt' and 'Lord Gordon' are popular old fiddle reels. 'Bonnie Kate' was composed by Daniel Dow of Perthshire, Scotland, around 1760. Michael Coleman from County Sligo recorded this tune in America in the 1920s. 'Lord Gordon' was composed by William Marshall, another Scottish fiddler, and he called it 'The Duke of Gordon's Rant'.

The Boyne Hunt

Johnny Doherty, a fiddler from Donegal tells how another reel, 'The Glen Road to Carrick', got its name:

I remember while I was a boy about 16 years of age. Our people, you see, they played at dances and weddings all over the county here. And of course there was a great session of fiddle playing at Glencolmcille every now and then. So we were coming out one fine day. We were just going back home to Glenfin and we had our fiddles in our cases. We started walking on the road out from Glencolmcille. Of course there was no other transport, you see, there was no way of travelling those days except to heel-and-toe. So we were coming out that long, lonely road there as you would come

from Cashel in Glencolmcille on out towards Carrick. So after a while two of the boys said,

'Ach, we'll make the road short. We'll take out the two fiddles and play a few good reels coming down the road.' Anyhow, they took out the two fiddles and this was the first reel that they played.

So my uncle, my mother's brother, who was a good fiddle-player, to tell the truth, says he,

'Boys! It's too bad there isn't a name for that tune!'

Says the other man, 'I'll tell you what we'll do. We'll call it "The Glen Road to Carrick".' And that's the name it has to this day!

The Glen Road to Carrick

Hornpipes

The hornpipe is a lovely solo dance. The rhythm is similar to a reel but it is played more slowly and usually has a lovely bounce to it. Hornpipes originated in England and are still a favourite with musicians in Northumberland. Many hornpipes, such as 'The High Level' and 'The Mathematician', are very difficult to play and performers sometimes use them to show how good they are!

The name hornpipe comes from a very old musical instrument. It was made of bone with fingerholes on the front. A reed was placed at one end, to blow into, then horns of cattle were secured at each end. In Scotland this was known as a stockhorn; in Wales, a pibcorn; and in England it was called a hornpipe.

The Boys of Bluehill

'The Boys of Bluehill' is a popular hornpipe played these days.

OTHER TYPES OF TUNES

There are many, many more varieties of tunes and dances.

Here are a few:

• Mazurka – a couple's dance originally from Poland; it is now popular in Counties Donegal and Down.

MAZURKA

Hugh Gillespie's Mazurka

• Polka – another dance from Europe; it became popular in Ireland in the late nineteenth century. County Kerry is well known for its lively polkas. When the dance came to Ireland many existing tunes were changed into polka rhythm in order to fit the new dance.

POLKA

All the Ways to Galway

• Strathspey – a kind of slow reel; it originated in North-East Scotland and is best played on the fiddle. You are more likely to hear strathspeys played in the northern counties of Ireland.

STRATHSPEY

The Iron Man

Other types of tunes you might come across are: waltz, highland or schottische, barn dance, german, planxty, lament, slow air, fling, set dance.

The Piper and The Pooka

This is a story about the Pooka, a supernatural creature that sometimes appears in the form of a goat.

A long time ago a piper called Pat lived in Dunmore in County Galway. He wasn't quite right in the head and people often made fun of him. He was very fond of good music but he was only able to play one tune on his pipes. This was a jig called 'The Black Rogue'. Even so, he played it well and he used to get a great deal of money from the gentlemen of Dunmore, for they enjoyed making a fool of him and his music.

The Black Rogue

One night Pat was coming home from a house dance. He had taken a bit too much to drink and staggered up the road carrying his pipes on his back. When he reached the little bridge near his mother's house he sat down, strapped on his pipes and began playing 'The Black Rogue'. Suddenly the Pooka appeared behind him. He grabbed poor Pat and hoisted him up on to his back. Pat grabbed hold of the Pooka's long horns and yelled into the creature's ear,

'Bad luck to you, nasty beast! Let me go home. I have a tenpenny bit for my mother and she is waiting for it.'

'Never mind your mother,' says the Pooka, 'but hold on tight. If you fall you'll break your neck and your pipes!'

Then says the beast, 'Less of this talking and play up for me "The Frost is All Over".'

'How can I play anything hanging on for dear life to your crooked horns?' wailed poor Pat.

'Well, we'll stop for a minute or two,' says the Pooka, 'and away you go with "The Frost is All Over".'

'I don't know that one,' says Pat.

'Never mind whether you do or you don't. Play up and I'll make you know it,' says the Pooka.

Pat the piper pumped air into the bag with his elbow and began playing. He played 'The Frost is All Over' in a grand style, much to his own amazement.

'My word, but you're a fine music-master,' says Pat to the Pooka. 'And will you tell me where it is that we are going?'

'There's a great feast in the house of the Banshee tonight, on the top of Croagh Patrick,' says the Pooka, 'and you'll be the piper.'

'You'll save me a journey then,' says Pat, 'for Father William gave that same journey to me to make amends for stealing his white gander!'

Again the Pooka hoisted Pat up on to his back. Pat hung on for dear life to the beast's horns as they rushed over bogs and hills. At last they reached the top of that great mountain, Croagh Patrick. The Pooka gave three loud thuds with one of his hoofs and a massive door opened in the mountain. In they both went to a fine hall. In the middle of the hall Pat saw a beautiful golden table. Around this table sat hundreds of very old women. One stood up.

'Welcome, Pooka of November! And who is this you have brought along?' she says.

'This is the best piper in Ireland!' says the Pooka.

Another old woman struck the ground with her blackthorn stick. A door opened in the wall, and what did Pat see coming out but the white gander he had stolen from Father William.

'Didn't my mother and I eat every bit of that very gander only last week!' exclaimed poor Pat.

The gander looked at Pat warily and proceeded to clean the golden table, fold it up and take it away. When the goose had gone the Pooka says to Pat,

'Now, strike up a tune on those pipes of yours for these ladies!'

So Pat began to play: reels, jigs, hornpipes, all sorts of tunes! He played 'The Pigeon on the Gate', 'The Boys of our Town', 'Over the Moor to Maggie', 'The Maid in the Meadow', 'The Stack of Barley' and tunes that he had never heard before, never mind tried to play. And the old women danced. They danced and danced until they dropped with exhaustion.

'Now is the time to pay the piper,' says the Pooka.

Every old woman took a gold piece from her purse and gave it to Pat.

'I'm as rich as the son of a lord!' cried Pat with glee.

'Come on now,' says the Pooka to Pat the piper, 'and I'll take you home.'

He handed Pat a beautiful new set of pipes, then hoisted him up on his back as before.

'Hold on tight,' he yells, and off they went with Pat hanging on to the Pooka's horns with one hand and holding tight to his old and new pipes with the other. After a while they reached the little bridge by Pat's mother's house at Dunmore.

'Go home now,' says the Pooka, 'along with the two things you never had before, sense and music.'

Away ran Pat up to the house and started banging on the door.

'Let me in, let me in!' he yelled, 'I'm as rich as a lord and the best piper in Ireland!!'

'You're drunk!' says his mother, opening the door.

'I am not,' says Pat, handing her the big bag of gold coins.

'Wait now, Mother,' he says, 'til you hear the music.'

Pat buckled on the new set of pipes and squeezed the bellows. Instead of music there came a noise as if all the ducks and geese in Ireland were screeching together. He wakened all the neighbours and up they came hammering on the cottage door, wanting to know what all the screeching was about. So Pat took off the new set of pipes and strapped on his old set. Out came beautiful, melodious music. Pat played 'The Geese in the Bog', 'The Bucks of Oranmore', 'The Fisherman's Lilt'. Everyone stared in amazement. So Pat told his story, all about his marvellous adventure with the Pooka.

Next morning, when his mother went to count the gold pieces all she found was a pile of leaves. Pat went to Father William and told his story, but the priest wouldn't believe a word of it. Nothing would do Pat until he played a tune for the priest. He buckled on the new pipes and as before the screeching began.

'Away with you, out of my sight, you thief!' shouts Father William, waving his arms at Pat. But Pat strapped on the old pipes to prove the truth of his story. He played 'Music in the Glen', 'Hand Me Down the Tackle' and 'The Lark on the Strand'.

And Pat continued to play wonderful music on his old pipes 'til the day he died and everyone said that he certainly was the best piper in Ireland!

CHAPTER FOUR

The Instruments

You can play traditional music on any instrument. However, some instruments are more suitable than others. Dance music has been played on the fiddle and pipes for hundreds of years. Other instruments such as the concertina and banjo are more recent. You are not likely to hear anyone play a jig or a reel on a trumpet or clarinet. Saxophones were popular instruments in céilí bands in the 1940s. Josie McDermott, a well-known flute player from County Roscommon, was also renowned for playing the saxophone.

THE FIDDLE

Here I come, poor slick slack,
My wife and family on my back
Five fingers on the fiddle
And five more on the griddle
Brave I am, there is no doubt
Well known here and round about.

from Traditional Christmas Rhymers Play

No one knows who first had the idea of using a bow on strings to make music, but throughout the world there are many examples of old fiddle-like instruments dating back to the tenth century, amongst them the morin-khuur of Mongolia, the erhu of China and rebec of Morocco. The earliest bowed instrument in the British Isles was called the 'crwyth' or 'crowd'. This instrument is mentioned in very old Irish poems.

In the fifteenth century a family of instruments known as viols was invented. These were bulky, violin-shaped instruments. The three largest, bass, tenor and treble, were played between the knees like the 'cello.

Viols were elegant instruments with a very distinct shape, narrow at the middle to allow the bow to be moved across the strings without hitting the sides of the instrument. Viols were the forerunners of the modern 'cello, viola and violin, three instruments which are played in orchestras today.

THE PARTS OF THE FIDDLE

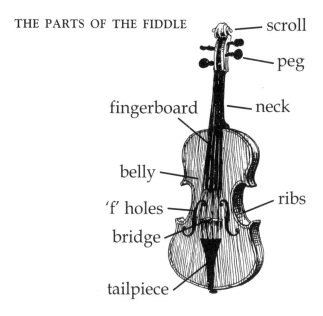

scroll

peg

fingerboard

neck

belly

'f' holes

ribs

bridge

tailpiece

The earliest known violin was made in Italy in 1549. This modern violin is the one used now to play traditional music. It came to Ireland around the year 1700 via Scotland, where there is also a great tradition of fiddle music.

The modern violin and the fiddle are one and the same instrument. Players of classical music tend to call their instrument a violin, while traditional musicians always call it a fiddle. Today the fiddle is the most popular instrument for playing traditional music and throughout Ireland there are hundreds of fiddle players.

The best fiddles are hand made and very good ones cost thousands of pounds. Each one consists of about eighty-four separate pieces of wood joined together.

Woods that make the best sound are chosen to make

violins. The back is made from a hardwood like maple or sycamore; a softwood such as pine or spruce is chosen for the front or belly. The neck and scroll are carved from a block of maple and the ribs are made from strips of maple or sycamore. Maple and pearwood purfling is inlaid around the back and belly of the instrument to prevent the wood splitting at the edges. It also gives a lovely decorative effect.

Harry Coulter

No nails or screws hold a violin together. Instead special glue is used. The colour of a violin depends on the varnish. Up to a dozen coats of varnish may be applied. This can take three or four months as each coat must be allowed to dry naturally. The ebony fingerboard, the pegs, the tailpiece and other fittings are then added to complete the instrument.

Hardiman the Fiddler

The Bow

The bow is a curved wooden stick, so called because the first bows were shaped like the ones used to shoot arrows. Stretched from the point to the frog are about 200 hairs from the tails of white horses. Sometimes other colours are used but these are bleached white. Nylon or other synthetic hair is used on cheap bows, but horsehair gives a better tone.

The bow is drawn across the strings to produce the sound. Before playing, rosin has to be put on the hairs of the bow. It is made from the sap of pine trees and you can buy it in a small, solid block. When it is rubbed on the hairs of the bow it leaves a sticky, powdery coating that allows the hairs to grip the strings and make a sound.

Strings

When fiddles were first played in Ireland fiddle strings were made from sheep gut. Nowadays traditional fiddlers use metal strings. Metal strings are much louder and stay in tune much better than gut strings.

Fiddle Styles

There are many different styles of fiddle-playing today (see Local Styles, Chapter One). Donegal, Kerry, East Galway, Clare and Antrim all have very distinctive styles. Lots of players have their own individual style of playing.

One of the best known and influential fiddle players was Michael Coleman of County Sligo. He was born in 1891 and emigrated to America at the age of 20. There he made many recordings of Irish fiddle music. Although he died in 1945, people still enjoy these recordings and try to copy his fast, smooth, Sligo style. One Clare fiddler, Patrick Kelly, said that the worst thing that ever happened to the West Clare fiddling style was the recordings of Michael Coleman. Lots of people gave up playing altogether when they heard them and others began trying to copy him.

THE PIPES

My name is Cash the piper
And I'm seen at race and fair
I'm known to all the jolly soul
From Wicklow to Kildare.

(popular nineteenth-century song)

Bagpipes are a very ancient instrument. No one knows when exactly they were first played but it was over a thousand

The Biniou

years ago. Every country in Europe has its own brand of bagpipes, e.g. the Zampogna in Italy, the Biniou in Brittany (France), the Northumbrian pipes in England, the Highland pipes in Scotland.

To play the bagpipes a bag is filled with air; this air is then pushed through a pipe, called the chanter, which has a reed inside. In Scottish or Highland bagpipes the air is blown into the bag by the mouth, but in Irish pipes the bag is blown up by bellows held under the elbow. The Gaelic word for elbow is 'uille', so these pipes are called uillean pipes. They are also known as union pipes. They were developed in Ireland in the eighteenth century.

THE PARTS OF THE PIPES

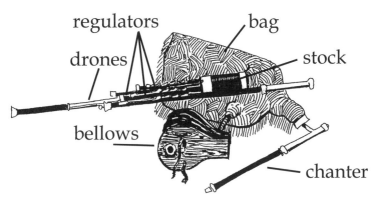

regulators bag

drones stock

bellows

chanter

Uillean pipers must sit down to play. The melody is played on the chanter. This pipe has seven fingerholes on the front and a thumbhole at the back. The chanter is usually made from ebony or boxwood and has a double reed to make the sound. A double reed consists of two small pieces of cane bound together. Early reeds for uillean pipes were made from elder, a common, native, Irish tree.

The chanter is held against the knee on a piece of leather called a popping strap. However, when the bottom note on the chanter is being played, the piper lifts up the chanter so that the bottom is open.

Paddy the Piper.

The drones sit across the piper's knee, behind the chanter. Most sets of uillean pipes have three wooden drones: small or tenor, middle or baritone and big or bass drone. Each of these has a single reed, i.e. one piece of cane, and sounds a note continuously in tune with the chanter. In the mouth-blown highland pipes, the drones lie against the piper's shoulder.

The regulators are a unique feature of uillean pipes. These three wooden pipes, tenor, baritone and bass, also sit across the piper's knee and each has a double reed like the chanter. Each one has four or five metal keys. While the tune is being

played on the chanter the piper can play the regulators by pressing on the keys with the wrist. In this way the regulators sound chords to accompany the tune being played on the chanter along with the continuous sound of the drones.

The Piper's Despair

Styles of Piping

There are two basic styles of playing the uillean pipes: open or tight. Open playing uses the least number of fingers needed to produce a note and tight playing uses as many as possible. Many players use a mixture of both methods and tend to develop their own personal styles of piping. Some pipers use the regulators a lot, others don't. Many pipers try to imitate the styles of legendary players such as Willie Clancy from County Clare.

A good set of uillean pipes is quite expensive to buy and this is one reason why there are more fiddlers and flute players than pipers. Pipes are also a very difficult instrument to learn. Nevertheless, in Ireland today there are hundreds of good pipers. Na Píobairí Uilleann is a society based in Dublin which promotes all aspects of piping.

Willie Clancy

THE TIN WHISTLE

The whistle is one of the earliest musical instruments. Throughout the world whistles have been made from bamboo, clay, reeds – out of any natural hollow tube. Bone whistles dating from the twelfth century have been dug up in Dublin.

The flageolet was a popular instrument in the seventeenth century. It had four finger holes on the front and two thumb holes at the back. In Old French 'flageolet' means little wind instrument. The tin whistle is sometimes called the flageolet, although it has six finger holes on the front and none at the back. The tin whistle is also called the penny whistle because it was and still is inexpensive to buy.

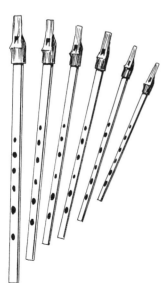

Most players use a whistle in the key of 'D', although you can buy them in other keys as well: from 'G', the smallest size (the smaller the whistle, the higher the pitch) through 'F', 'Eb' and 'C', to the biggest one in 'Bb'. Sometimes 'C' or 'Bb' whistles are used to play a slow air because they have a more mellow tone.

Mary Bergin of Dublin is one of Ireland's best known whistle players. She has a smooth, flowing style. Whistle players from the northern counties of Ireland, such as Willis Patton from County Antrim and Cathal McConnell from County Fermanagh, tend to have a much more breathy style. This style is not, however, confined to the North. Micho Russell of

Mouthpiece

Doolin, County Clare, also played in a distinctive breathy style. To produce a breathy style, individual notes are played with single toots instead of a continuous stream of air blown into the whistle.

The tin whistle is a very simple instrument and many people learn their first tune on one. Nevertheless, it is a difficult instrument to play really well.

Casey the Whistler

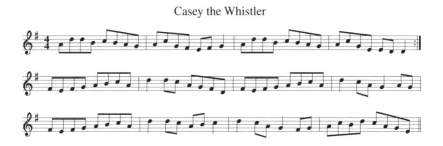

THE FLUTE

The flute is basically a long hollow tube. It is made of wood, usually rosewood or African blackwood. It has six finger holes like the tin whistle, but unlike the whistle, air is blown across the mouthpiece to produce the sound. Sometimes four, six or eight holes covered by metal keys are added to produce extra notes. Traditional musicians don't use these keys very often and sometimes block the holes up.

The flute was a favourite gentleman's instrument in the  'big houses' of Ireland at the end of the eighteenth century. When the modern silver flute was developed in the middle of the nineteenth century classical musicians no longer wanted to play the wooden flute. Some of these wooden instruments undoubtedly found their way into the hands of 'ordinary' folk, who began playing traditional music on them.

Now the flute is one of Irish music's most popular instruments and there are many different styles of playing. Counties Roscommon, Leitrim and Sligo are particularly well known for flute players. John McKenna of Leitrim had a very breathy, rhythmic style. He made a lot of recordings in America from 1921 to 1937. Matt Molloy of Roscommon, a member of the world-famous group The Chieftains, has a smooth flowing

Frankie Kennedy

style. County Fermanagh also has a very strong flute-playing tradition. Eddie Duffy was a fine player who had some unusual tunes and was a great influence on players such as Cathal McConnell.

The wooden flute has a lovely mellow tone and is often played as a solo instrument. Fiddle and flute together are a great combination, although the flute sounds well with any instrument.

THE HARP

The harp is a very ancient instrument. Pictures of harps can be seen on High Crosses at Monasterboice, County Louth, and Castledermot, County Kildare. Harps are often mentioned in old Irish legends. Here is one:

The Harp of the Dagda*

The Tuatha De Danann, or the fairy folk of the goddess Danu, were celebrating their victory over the Fomorians at the Battle of Moytura, and had gathered for a great feast in the banquet hall of their castle. Someone called for the Dagda to play some music on his harp. He went to fetch it, but discovered that his magical instrument had been stolen by the Fomorians. Ogma and Lugh jumped up from their feast, declaring that they would get it back. So, these two champions set out with the Dagda to pursue the Fomorians.

They travelled all night and all the following day, climbing nine heathery hills and crossing nine dark valleys and nine broad rivers. At last they found the Fomorians' camp in a

dismal glen. And there among them lay the harp of the Dagda. None of the Fomorians had the power to play this magical harp no matter how hard he or she tried. Only the Dagda could draw out any music. When the Dagda spied his harp he called out,

'Come summer, come winter,

Mouths of harps and bags and pipes.'

Magically the harp sprang up. Nine Fomorians were killed as it flew through the air to the arms of the Dagda. Ogma and Lugh begged him to play. So the Dagda began. First he played 'goltraí', sorrowful music, and the three champions watched the Fomorians weep. Then he played 'geantraí', joyful music. The men shouted while the women laughed and danced to the magical strings. Then the Dagda played 'suantraí', the music of sleep. The Fomorians all slipped into a deep sleep induced by the soothing, enchanting music of the harp. And the Dagda, Ogma and Lugh returned to the Tuatha De Danann.

* Dagda: the god of magic in Celtic legend

For many centuries harpers were respected members of Irish society and played music to accompany poetry recited by bards. The Brian Boru harp, which is kept at Trinity College, Dublin, would have been used to play this ancient

music. It is the oldest surviving example of an Irish harp, dating back to the fourteenth century.

As early Irish society changed, this ancient bardic music died out. Harpers became travelling musicians, depending on rich lords to feed them and give them places to stay, in return for music.

The best known of these wandering minstrels, who were often blind and had no other way of earning a living, was Turlough O'Carolan (1670-1738). He composed over two hundred pieces of music and many are still played today, not only by harpers, but by fiddlers and pipers: tunes such as 'O'Carolan's Concerto', 'Planxty* Irwin', 'Bridget Cruise', 'Planxty Charles O'Connor'. Shortly before he died on 25 March 1738 O'Carolan called for his harp and played 'O'Carolan's Farewell to Music'.

Planxty: a piece of music in honour of someone.

Planxty Irwin

After the death of O'Carolan, harp music was in danger of dying out altogether. However, in 1791 the Belfast Harp Society was established and a famous festival was held the following year. The first prize was 10 guineas and was won

Barbara Haugh

by Charles Fanning, a harper from County Cavan. The oldest player there was Denis Hempson, aged 97 years, from Magilligan, County Derry, and the youngest was a 15-year-old boy from County Armagh named William Carr.

The Belfast Harp Orchestra was formed by harper Janet Harbison for the 200th anniversary of the Belfast Harp Festival, proving that the tradition of harp playing in Ireland has not died out.

The Irish harp is much smaller than the concert harp played in an orchestra. It has fewer strings and no tuning peddles. Depending on what is being played, the tuning of the Irish harp can be altered by using a special key to turn the

Strike the Gay Harp

pegs where the strings are attached. Tightening a string makes it sound higher while loosening one lowers the sound.

If you were to go to a session of Irish music today it is highly unlikely that you would see or hear a harp. They are more commonly played in concerts, in much the same way as they have been for hundreds of years.

The best known and respected harper today is Derek Bell, who plays with the world-famous group The Chieftains.

THE BANJO

The first banjos were made of gourds. A gourd is a large fruit with a hard skin, e.g. a marrow or melon. The flesh was scraped out and the hollow shell used as a sound box. A wooden neck and horsehair strings were added. Instruments

like these were played in Africa and the West Indies in the 1600s, and African slaves brought them to America. There the gourd was replaced by a wooden rim covered with animal skin. Gradually the banjo has developed into the complicated and beautiful instrument we have today.

The banjo was seen for the first time in Ireland in 1845, when the Virginia Minstrels visited with their musical show. They painted their faces black and strummed banjos as they sang. The leader

of the Virginia minstrels was Joel Sweeney of Buckingham County, Virginia. His ancestors were from County Mayo.

The tenor banjo, as used to play Irish music, has four steel strings. Most players tune their instrument like a fiddle: E,A,D,G, and use a plectrum to sound the strings.

One of the first recordings of traditional Irish music on the banjo was made in America in the 1920s by Mike Flanagan of County Waterford. But the banjo never really became popular in Ireland until Barney McKenna recorded with The Dubliners in the 1960s.

Ring the Banjo

THE HAMMER DULCIMER

The dulcimer is a member of the zither family of instruments. Various examples of the instrument are found all over the world, e.g. in Greece, the santouri; in Switzerland, the hackbrett; in Hungary, the cembalon; in China, the yangchyn.

The hammer dulcimer is a trapezium-shaped sound box with wire strings. These are played with wooden hammers, hence the name hammer or hammered dulcimer. Sometimes pieces of leather or wool are stuck to the hammers to soften the tone. The dulcimer produces a loud ringing sound and is best played as a solo instrument.

John Rea

The hammer dulcimer is a very popular instrument in the USA. Players such as Jim Couza and Bill Fennig play a wide variety of music on the instrument, from Irish reels and jigs to jazz, classical, and country and western. In Ireland, however, the hammer dulcimer has never been particularly popular.

Undoubtedly the best-known player of traditional music on the hammer dulcimer was John Rea, of Glenarm, County Antrim. John was born into a very musical family. His father and six brothers all played the fiddle and another brother, Willie, also played the dulcimer. John worked and lived on a tug-boat in Belfast Lough and often spent his evenings playing in Pat's Bar at the docks in Belfast. He used to balance the dulcimer on top of a matchbox on a table. This let the bottom of the instrument vibrate, giving a much richer sound.

THE JAW'S HARP

The Jaw's harp or trump is another ancient instrument found in many countries throughout the world. In Dublin some jaw's harps made of wood and bone were discovered at an archaeological site. These turned out to be over a thousand years old. Today, however, the jaw's harp is made from brass or iron.

The lyre-shaped frame is held against the lips with one hand, leaving the pronged, narrow blade or tongue free to be

John Campbell playing the jaw's harp

moved or twanged with the other hand. The player uses his breath and cheeks to change the notes. The mouth cavity acts like a resonator and makes the sounds louder, in the same way as the soundbox of a guitar or fiddle. It is an inexpensive little instrument, costing little over a pound. Surprisingly it is not played by very many people.

THE MOUTH ORGAN

The mouth organ works by blowing air across metal reeds to produce sounds. Like the tin whistle, each instrument plays in a certain key,

and like the tin whistle it is cheap and easy to obtain. However, it is by no means a popular instrument for Irish music. The Murphys from County Wexford are probably the best-known players. Brendan Power and Eddie Clarke have also recorded Irish music on the mouth organ.

THE CONCERTINA

The concertina is a small, hexagonal-shaped, button-keyed instrument. It works like a mouth organ. Instead of the air being blown by the mouth, the concertina uses bellows to push the air through the metal reeds to produce the sound. It was invented by an Englishman, Charles Wheatstone, in 1829. At first he called it the symphonium and later this instrument became known as the English concertina.

At the same time, in Germany, Carl Friedrich Uhlig produced a similar instrument which he called the

Konzertina. English makers developed this instrument into the one we know today as the Anglo-concertina; and this is the one that Irish musicians favour. The English concertina is not played in Ireland. The difference between the two instruments is quite simple. When you press one of the keys of the English concertina, the note produced when you push in the bellows is the same as the one sounded when you pull them out. The Anglo-concertina sounds different notes on push and pull.

It didn't take long for the concertina to become popular in Ireland. The first mention of one is around 1850, and by 1860

Jason O'Rourke, concertina,
and Ian Hull, bodhrán

it was a common instrument in County Clare. English sailors are reputed to have brought it when sailing to and from the Shannon Estuary. One of the main reasons for its popularity was because as a County Clare player remembers: 'Concertinas were cheap then (1898). You could get the smaller one for 2/6 (13p), and the large one cost 6/6 (33p), and if you minded it, it would last a few years, anyway, with constant playing.'

The situation is somewhat different today. Good quality concertinas are hard to find and cost several hundred pounds.

The first recording of traditional Irish music on the concertina was made in America by William Mulally from County Westmeath in 1926.

Michael Rooney

The concertina is still a very popular instrument in County Clare, although players can be heard in every other county in Ireland as well.

The Concertina Reel

The attraction of the concertina is its pleasant, mild tone that blends well with other instruments.

ACCORDIONS

Accordions were developed in the nineteenth century and come in many shapes, sizes and keys. The main ones used to play traditional music are the melodeon, the button accordion and the piano-keyed accordion. The oldest of these, the melodeon, has ten buttons on one side for playing the melody and two buttons for playing bass notes with the other hand. There are few melodeon players today, as many tunes are too complicated to play on an instrument with such a small range of notes.

The two-row button accordion was developed from the melodeon by adding a second row of buttons for the melody hand and several more bass notes. The two-row button accordion or 'box' as it is known, is the most popular in this family of instruments and there are two distinctive styles of

Caroline Judge

playing. The 'push and pull' or 'press and draw' style uses accordions with one row of buttons in the key of C# and the other row in D. This is the C#/D accordion. D/D# accordions are also played in this very rhythmic style. Jackie Daly is a very well-known 'push and pull' style player.

The other style of box playing is very smooth and flowing and uses the B/C accordion. Joe Burke is probably the best-known player in this style.

The piano-keyed accordion is sometimes used in Irish music. It is a popular instrument in céilí bands.

ACCOMPANIMENT

In recent times a great variety of instruments have come to be used as an accompaniment in traditional Irish music. These are instruments that do not play the melody of a tune but, like the regulators on uillean pipes or the bass buttons of an accordion, can enhance the melody or rhythm.

The Piano

The piano gives céilí bands their distinctive sound. The rhythmic 'vamping' helps the musicians keep a steady beat for the dancers. Pianos were used in  early fiddle recordings in America and they are quite popular with some fiddlers today. Two notable piano players are Josephine Keegan and Charlie Lennon. Both are fine fiddlers as well, so they have a deep understanding of Irish dance music.

The Guitar

The guitar is a very versatile instrument. It plays a major part in every type of music today, from pop and rock to jazz and classical music. In traditional music simple chord accompaniment is possible. More accomplished players such as Arty McGlynn and Steve Cooney are in great demand, especially when it comes to performing on stage or in a recording studio.

Davy Graham

The Bouzouki

This is a nineteenth-century Greek instrument. It has four sets of double metal strings and was introduced to Irish music in the 1960s by Johnny Moynihan of the group

Ciaran Curran playing the cittern

Sweeney's Men. Since then a number of similar instruments have appeared, such as the cittern and the mandola. Donal Lunny and Alec Finn are two well-known bouzouki players.

The Bodhrán

The bodhrán is a shallow, one-sided drum played with a stick or the hand. It is usually made of goat skin, stretched over a wooden rim. It is possible that the word is derived from tambourine. In Sligo, jingles are sometimes added, making it sound more like a tambourine. At the beginning of this century the bodhrán was played by Christmas Rhymers as they travelled from house to house with their mumming plays. It was also played by the Wren Boys on St Stephen's Day in Dingle, County Kerry. In the 1960s it became a popular accompaniment to Irish music.

Ciaran Brady

The Bones

These are two cow ribs boiled and dried. They are rattled together like castanets. Sometimes 'bones' made of wood or slate are used. Spoons have a similar effect. All are very loud.

The Magic Fiddle

There is an old belief that if you discover a wild rose with a double root you can use it to obtain magical powers. At dawn on Mayday or All Saints Day (1st November), go to the place where the wild rose grows, take off all your clothes and crawl beneath the roots calling to the fairies for the power of magic. This is a story about a man who did just that.

There was once a man called Jack, who loved music, but he couldn't play a single tune no matter what instrument he tried. And he had tried every one that he could lay his hands on – pipes, fiddle, concertina, banjo and flute. Now Jack had heard the old story about the double-rooted wild rose and off he went in search of one. He was very determined to gain magical musical powers. He tramped through fields, crawled through hedges and clambered over ditches. He tore his clothes, cut his hands and fell into muddy pools. But he never gave up. At last, in a lonely field he found one growing in a hawthorn hedge.

One misty morning after a dark, ghostly Halloween night he went to the magic bush, took off all his clothes and called out to the fairies for the gift of music. When he turned to put his clothes back on, what did he find lying on them but a strange looking fiddle with only one string. Eagerly he drew the bow across the string. Out came the greatest music he had ever heard! Jack was overjoyed. His wish had been granted.

From that day on Jack went to all the dances, fairs, weddings and céilís in the district and everybody loved his lively music, even though the fiddle played only one tune. People said that they would rather listen to that one tune all night than all the reels, jigs and hornpipes in the world.

One day Jack was playing his magic one-stringed fiddle at a country fair. A crowd gathered around him to enjoy the music. Among the crowd was a foreign-looking gentleman. He waited until everyone else had gone and then told Jack that he had come to Ireland to buy horses for the King of France.

'Would you come along with me and play for the King of France?' the gentleman asked. Now Jack was always ready for a bit of adventure and excitement so he said that he surely would. He set off with the foreign gentleman and all the horses he had bought. Away over the sea to France they sailed.

Jack's Delight

For twenty years Jack stayed at the court of the King of France. And every night, for twenty years, he played the same tune on his magic fiddle. No one ever tired of that magical tune. In fact the more they heard it the more keen they were to hear it again. And no one else could play the strange one-stringed fiddle. Great musicians of France tried to play music on the instrument, but all they got were horrible screeching and scraping noises. It was a great mystery to them, but of course they didn't know about the double-rooted briar and the magic of Irish fairies.

One night everyone in the palace was fast asleep, except of course the palace guards. Suddenly, a loud ringing sound began, just like the plucking of fiddle strings. It was so loud that the King himself woke up. The sound grew louder and louder until it was like thunder. The guards searched the palace to find the cause of the weird noises. They came to Jack's room. The great ringing seemed to be there. They broke down the door. Poor Jack was lying dead in his bed and the fiddle, which was usually hanging on the wall over his bed, was broken into a thousand pieces on the floor. The wonderful music of Jack and his magic fiddle would never be heard again.

Jack Won't Sell His Fiddle

CHAPTER FIVE

Past Masters

Johnny McFadden and Jeannie McAllister
from County Antrim

Throughout the long history of traditional Irish music there have been thousands of players. Some simply played a few tunes at local parties and dances. Others travelled the length and breadth of Ireland meeting musicians and learning new tunes. Many more travelled further afield to America, Australia and England. Some made invaluable recordings, still available today.

All of these musicians, whether they stayed at home or travelled widely, had an influence on the musicians that came after them. Obviously there were so many great musicians in the past that it is impossible to mention them all. Here we focus briefly on five of the greats: Micho Russell, Pádraig O'Keeffe, Joe Holmes, William Mulally and Séamus Ennis.

Margaret Barry playing the banjo

MICHO RUSSELL

Micho Russell was born in Dunagore, Doolin, County Clare, an area well known for traditional music. His mother played the concertina and the single-row melodeon and his father was a singer. His aunt and uncle were also involved in music so there was no shortage of encouragement for him to play.

Micho Russell

Micho began playing the tin whistle at the age of eleven. He said that it took him fourteen or fifteen years playing before he made any headway! He left school when he was fourteen and from then on worked as a farmer in Doolin. For a long time he played music with his brothers, Pakie on the concertina and Gus on the flute.

Micho also played the flute and was a good singer. He was an easy going, good humoured man and this showed in his whistle-playing. He had a simple style that was unhurried and melodic with lots of interesting variations. He never cluttered tunes with too many notes. Above all, he enjoyed playing. He was a well-travelled musician and made many trips abroad. He was recorded many times for television and radio. Tragically, Micho was killed in a car accident in 1994.

PÁDRAIG O'KEEFFE

Pádraig O'Keeffe was born in October 1887 in Glentaun, County Kerry. He was fortunate to come from a very musical family. His mother, Margaret, was a fine concertina player and singer. She also played the

fiddle and her brother, Pádraig's uncle, Cal O'Callaghan, was also a fiddler, with a wonderful store of tunes. Pádraig's father, John, was a school teacher and, although he didn't play an instrument himself, he encouraged his children to play and study music. Pádraig spent a lot of time at his Uncle Cal's house learning tunes and songs.

Pádraig O'Keeffe

When he grew up, Pádraig became a teacher, taking over his father's job as local schoolmaster in Glentaun. But it wasn't very long before he decided that school teaching was not for him. He took up teaching of a different kind and became a travelling fiddle teacher. He travelled twenty or thirty miles a day. Sometimes he walked, sometimes he went by bicycle and occasionally he rode on a donkey. Over the years he taught hundreds of fiddle players using his own method of writing music that was easier to follow than the usual way. Some of his pupils are very well-known fiddle players, including Denis Murphy, Julia Clifford and Paddy Cronin.

Pádraig O'Keefe was very highly respected in his neighbourhood. He was a kind-hearted man with a great sense of humour as well as being a wonderful fiddle player.

He died during an exceptionally cold spell in February 1963 aged 75 years.

As I Went Out upon the Ice

JOE HOLMES

Joe Holmes was born at Killyrammer, near Ballymoney, County Antrim, on 6 February 1906. His grandfather was a fiddle player and his mother, Jane, was a fine singer. The house where he was brought up was well known as a céilí house in the area. The door was always open and musicians, singers, storytellers and dancers often called in. Both Joe and his elder brother Harry became fiddlers and they learned many tunes from musicians who called at the house, as well as from their grandfather. Harry brought Joe a fiddle back from France when he returned from fighting in the First World War.

Joe left school at the age of fourteen and one of the first jobs he had was carrying the red flag in front of a steamroller doing roadworks. Throughout his life he had many other jobs, often connected with the making of linen. Indeed, many lint-pullings were held at his house. These were big parties held for all the people who helped with the flax harvest. These parties could last all night long!

Joe often played the Doctor with the Christmas Rhymers, who travelled from house to house in the district:

> *Doctor: I am your Doctor pure and good*
> *With my medicine I'll stop his blood,*
> *If you must have this man's life saved*
> *Full fifty guineas I must receive.*

> *St George: What can you cure, Doctor?*

Doctor: I can cure anything within the plague with-
  out,
The palsy or the gout.
Rather more if you bring to me
An old woman of three score and ten
With the knuckle bone of her big toe broke,
I can fix it up again.

St George: What is your cure, Doctor?

Doctor: My cure is hen's pens, peasy weasy,
Turkey's treacle, midge's oil, the juice of the poker,
The sap of the tongs, two turkey eggs two feet long,
All mixed up in a hen's bladder,
And stirred up with a Tom-cat's feather.
I carry a small bottle in my hip-coat, waist-coat pocket,
Which contains hokey mokers, elegant pain,
Taste this dead man and fight again ...

In the 1960s Joe met traditional singer Len Graham, and they struck up a great musical friendship. For many years they travelled throughout Ireland, singing, lilting and making music wherever they went.

Joe Holmes was a warm, friendly man. His gentleness and joy of life were expressed through his music. He died suddenly in January 1978.

The Hen's Schottische

WILLIAM MULALLY

For many years Irish music played on the concertina has been closely associated with County Clare. But the first recordings on this instrument were made by a player from County Westmeath, William Mulally.

William, or Willie as he was known, was born in Milltown in February 1884. Although his father and mother were not musicians, Willie and his six brothers and four sisters all played. Among the instruments they played were uillean pipes,

William Mulally

flute, whistle, mouth organ and of course concertina. Willie's first teacher was a neighbour, Mrs Heydune. In Westmeath at that time concertina playing was very popular and Willie often played at house dances.

Willie, like his father, became a carpenter and at the age of 21 he went to live and work in England. He stayed there for a few years and then travelled on to America where he joined the Army. When his time in the Army ended, he moved to New York to be with his brother, Michael, and it was here that the first recordings of his music were made. During the following year, 1927, Willie made his final recordings. After this Willie was seldom seen or heard of. He left his concertina with a nephew in Philadelphia and never returned for it. His family had little contact with him and he died somewhere in America almost thirty years later.

SÉAMUS ENNIS

There are many great names in the world of Irish piping. Séamus Ennis is one of the greatest and, although he was not

Séamus Ennis

a teacher, he has had a huge influence on all uillean pipers playing today. Ask any piper about music and the name Séamus Ennis is sure to be mentioned!

Séamus was born in Jamestown, County Dublin in 1919. His mother was a fiddler and his father was a well-known piper. Growing up with music in the air it is not surprising that young Séamus began playing himself. He started on the pipes when he was thirteen years old and had lessons with his father. He spent his whole life, from this time onwards, devoted to music, collecting tunes and songs from musicians all over Ireland for the Irish Folklore Commission and the BBC. He was often heard on radio and, later, on television. As well as being a great piper he was an excellent whistle player and singer. He had a wonderful way with words and had a wealth of jokes, folktales and stories, often about music. One such story that he heard on his travels in County Galway is about a piping competition. It is called 'Henry Bohannon'. Séamus died in October 1982 at Naul, County Dublin.

A Story told by Séamus Ennis: Henry Bohannon

Long ago there was a man called Henry Bohannon. He was trying to play the pipes but was not making a good job of it at all. He lived beside the sea and every day he went fishing for his dinner. One afternoon he was sitting on a rock dangling his fishing line in the sea. He was very sad and had a big long face on him. A little man appeared beside him and asked,

'Henry, why are you always so sad?' Henry heaved a big sigh and explained how he was trying to play the pipes but couldn't quite get the hang of it.

'Well,' said the wee man, 'that's easily fixed. Which would you like, music to please yourself and nobody else, or music to please everybody but yourself?'

'Oh,' replied Henry. 'I think I'd rather have music to please myself, never mind anyone else'.

'OK,' said the little man. 'Tonight, at home, strap on the pipes just before midnight. When the clock strikes twelve you will be able to play the most wonderful music that will please yourself no end.' So Henry did just this. The clock struck midnight and he played what he thought was the loveliest music. He was very happy. But nobody else seemed to enjoy his music. Anytime he played, no one took any notice so it wasn't long 'til his sad face returned.

A few weeks later Henry was sitting on the rocks fishing for his tea when the little man sat down beside him again.

'I see that your sad face is back again,' he said. 'Is it the music?'

'Yes,' replied Henry.

'Well,' said the little man, 'I'll give you another chance. This time, when you play the pipes at midnight you'll play music to please everybody but yourself.' And with that, the little man was gone.

Night time came. Henry strapped on the pipes, blew up the bag with the bellows and as the clock struck twelve began to play. Well, in a few days everyone was talking about Henry Bohannon and what a great piper he had turned out to be. His fame spread and he was invited to play in all the big houses of the gentry. He became resident piper for a wealthy nobleman. Now this nobleman was very proud of his piper and was forever boasting about him. He happened to be over in London one time. He was visiting another nobleman who also had a piper.

'What do you think of my piper?' said the English nobleman to the Irish nobleman.

'Oh, not much', said the Irish nobleman. 'I have a piper at home that could play rings round him'.

An argument started and eventually the English nobleman bet the Irish nobleman that his piper was better than his. So Henry Bohannon was sent for. After a few days he

arrived in London. In those days you had to be a good piper to become a nobleman's resident piper, so the competition depended on the number of tunes you could play. The contest began and the two pipers played tune for tune against each other all night until neither of them had a tune left. Henry took off the pipes and stepped outside for a breath of dawn air. As he stood outside trying to remember another tune he heard a lark singing above him in the sky. He listened to the lark's song, went back inside, strapped on the pipes and played 'The Lark in the Morning'. And so it was that Henry Bohannon won the competition and the Irish nobleman won the bet.

When Sick is it Tea You Want?

CHAPTER SIX

Present Players

The musicians of Ireland are as harmless and inoffensive a
class of persons as ever existed and there can be no greater
proof of this than the very striking fact that in the criminal
statistics of the country the name of an Irish piper or
fiddler has scarcely, if ever, been known to appear.

Captain Francis O'Neill, in *Irish Minstrels and Musicians*, 1913

In the following pages you will read about some musicians
who play traditional Irish music today. All come from
different backgrounds. Some come from musical families.
Others do not. They have learned their music in different

ways and have been influenced
by a great variety of musicians.
Some can read music, some
cannot. The one thing that they
all have in common is a great
love of music and a dedication
to their art. And this is all
anyone needs to play Irish

Jim McGrath, accordion, and
Charlie Woods, fiddle

music. At first it is hard work: learning about your
instrument, learning the necessary skills, learning and
practising tunes. But hard work can be enjoyable. And the

reason why traditional Irish music has continued for hundreds of years is because it is fun. People enjoy listening. People enjoy playing.

JOHN HUGHES

John Hughes discovered traditional music when he was twelve years old. He had wanted to play the flute since he was a small boy and his wish came true when he joined the orchestra of Glengormley Secondary School. Meanwhile he was learning tunes on the tin whistle from Kevin McLaverty, a friend of his father's. Kevin also played the uillean pipes. John has been fascinated by the pipes ever since. He is now an accomplished piper himself, although he rarely plays the pipes in public. Soon John left the school orchestra and concentrated on playing traditional music. As there weren't many traditional musicians living nearby, he had to learn tunes off records. He says himself that he is not good at reading music and prefers learning by ear.

One record that had a great influence on him was a BBC recording made in 1967 called 'Ulster's Flowery Vale'. It featured the flute playing of County Fermanagh man Cathal McConnell.

The first music sessions that John went to were held in a hall in Troopers Lane, Carrickfergus, County Antrim. John's father had actually started up this session with two friends six years earlier. John also travelled to the regular Saturday night session at Balloo House, Killinchy, County Down, where the main instrument was the fiddle. He travelled further afield too, listening, absorbing and learning tunes all the time. A spell at the Ulster Polytechnic at Jordanstown introduced him to another circle of musicians. John became a member of the group Drumlin. They played their own brand of traditional tunes and songs at various folk clubs and festivals and eventually recorded a tape.

Now aged thirty-five, John is a mature and sensitive musician. He enjoys playing in sessions and on stage and travels widely to hear and play music.

One of his favourite tunes is 'The Gooseberry Bush', a reel which he says gave him a lot of trouble to learn.

The Gooseberry Bush

GERRY O'CONNOR

Gerry O'Connor, of Dundalk, County Louth, comes from a very musical family. His seven uncles are all musicians and his mother, Rose, is an accomplished fiddle player. She is renowned throughout Ireland as a teacher of traditional fiddle. She taught all her children to play and Gerry started at the age of five. He enjoyed playing and practising and from the age of eleven was winning competitions, including All Ireland titles and, later, The Fiddler of Oriel.

Gerry O'Connor

As well as playing the fiddle for a living, Gerry is also a fiddle maker. He says that he makes about six instruments each year. He tours the world as a member of the group Skylark and along with his wife, Eithne, Gerry plays in Lá Lugh, a group that specialises in the music and song of County Louth.

Gerry is a very skilful fiddle player. He plays with flair and originality and has the reputation of having the best bow-arm in Ireland!

You can hear Gerry on many recordings, such as: 'Skylark', Claddagh Records; 'Skylark: All of It', Claddagh

A tune from Gerry

The Eel in the Sink

Records; 'Skylark: Light and Shade', Claddagh Records; 'Cosa gan Bhróga', a recording made for Gael Linn Records with Eithne Ní Uallacháin and Dessie Wilkinson; 'Lá Lugh', Claddagh Records 1993; 'Brighid's Kiss, Lá Lugh-Lughnasa' Music 1996.

TOM McGONIGLE

Tom comes originally from Omagh, County Tyrone, but his interest in music did not develop until he moved to Newcastle, County Down, at the age of ten. Shortly afterwards he began playing the piano accordion. He went to Sunday afternoon sessions of music and began picking up tunes from local musicians such as Barney Farrell on the piano accordion, fiddlers Peter Gallagher and Harry Polland and banjo player Billy Redmond. He got plenty of encouragement from friends and family and continued playing the piano accordion for six years. On a trip to Donegal he was introduced to the concertina as he had forgotten to bring his accordion. He immediately took to the instrument and bought a cheap one for himself. He now plays an eighty-year old Jeffries concertina which has a lovely mellow tone.

Tom McGonigle

Tom continued to soak up traditional music after he left school and went to university at Coleraine. There was a lot of music around Portstewart and Portrush and Tom learned many tunes during this time. On his trips home he played with Monaghan fiddler Pat McKenna and also regularly at sessions with Gus McIlroy, another fiddler of Drumnaquoile, County Down.

Unlike a lot of musicians today, Tom likes to play tunes at a moderate speed so that none of the melody is lost to the listener.

He now lives, works and plays music in Belfast. You can hear him on 'Road Map of Ireland', a recording made by Outlet Records in 1981 with whistle player Robert McGouran.

One of Tom's favourite tunes

Tit for Tat

GEORDIE McADAM

Geordie has loved traditional music since he was a boy growing up on the Shankill Road in Belfast. He began playing the flute at the age of thirteen and has been a member of various flute bands ever since. He currently plays with the Ballywalter Flute Band who have twice been world champions.

Geordie McAdam

In 1967 Geordie and a few friends started up a folk group on the Shankill Road after hearing the well-known group The Dubliners. They sang the same songs and learned all the tunes but the sound wasn't quite right without a fiddle, so Geordie tried his hand at it and has been playing one ever since. He became a familiar face at music sessions in and around Belfast. Over the years he has travelled the length and breadth of Ireland playing and enjoying the music. After

Jumping Geordie

moving to live in Bangor his regular music sessions were at Comber and Killinchy, although both these sessions have now stopped.

These days Geordie is better known as a player of Old Timey American music and is the fiddler with Appalachian Strings. Now he is more likely to go to Kentucky than Kilkenny to hear a bit of music. He is a great all-round musician and a mine of information on any subject from fishing to UFOs. He is one of the few craftsmen left working with stained glass.

Geordie can be heard on two recordings made by the group Fluters Five, on 'Pick'n'Choose' recorded by the Black Mountain String Band in 1994, and on 'Appalachian Strings' recorded in 1997.

CAROLINE JUDGE

Caroline Judge is from St Albans, England. One day, at the age of nine, she picked up a button accordion that happened to be in the house and began messing around on it. She has been playing the instrument ever since. Her parents are originally from Ireland. Both enjoy traditional music and they encouraged her to play. She began going to a music teacher in Luton every week. Eventually her father, Pat Judge, started a branch of Comhaltas Ceoltóirí Éireann (CCÉ) in St Albans and music classes for children began closer to home. Caroline's three sisters all play traditional music as well.

By the time she was nineteen years old, Caroline had won the All Ireland title five times on the single-row melodeon and once on the two-row button accordion. She also played in St Colmcille's Céilí Band that won the All Ireland title in 1988 and 1990.

Caroline learned to read music at primary school and found it useful when she was learning the accordion. Now, like most musicians, she learns tunes by ear. Over the years she has enjoyed listening and playing with different musicians in sessions and festivals both in England and Ireland. The recordings of Joe Cooley had a great influence on her style while she was learning.

Caroline now lives in Belfast and plays regularly at sessions and for set dancing. She can be heard on the 1981

A tune from Caroline

The Morning Mist

recording made by the CCÉ group that toured America and Canada. St Colmcille's Céilí Band has also made two recordings of dance music: 'Across the Water' and 'Lovely Hurling'.

ROBBIE HANNAN

Robbie Hannon

Robbie was born in 1961 and lives in Holywood, County Down. He now works there as curator of music in the Ulster Folk and Transport Museum. He became interested in traditional music as a boy through listening to his parents' collection of Irish music records. When he was thirteen he began playing the piano accordion, but as he says himself, he soon lost interest as he didn't find the instrument suitable for playing traditional music. The first pipers he heard were Paddy Moloney of The Chieftains, Liam O'Flynn of Planxty, and Paddy Keenan of The Bothy Band. He was fascinated by the sound of the pipes and at the age of fifteen began playing them himself. At this time he started visiting Fermanagh piper Seán McAloon who was living in Belfast. Seán gave him lots of hints and help on piping. Robbie learned a lot of music from him. Seán used to make the reeds for Robbie's 200-year old pipes.

When he was learning the pipes, Robbie listened intently to recordings of older pipers such as Séamus Ennis, Willie Clancy and Tommy Reck and these pipers had a strong influence on his style. In 1977 he attended piping classes in Milltown Malbay, County Clare. It was here that he first met piper Joe and fiddler Dermot McLaughlin from Derry and this was the beginning of a close musical relationship. Through the McLaughlins Robbie discovered the traditional music of Donegal. Donegal tunes form a large part of his repertoire.

Uillean pipes are a difficult instrument to master and through his natural talent and love for the instrument, Robbie is now one of the most respected pipers in Ireland. He has made the following recordings: 'The Piper's Rock', a compilation of young pipers made by Mulligan Records in 1978; 'Robbie Hannan: Traditional Music Played on the Uillean Pipes', Claddagh Records 1990; 'Rabharta Ceoil (In Full Spate)', Donegal fiddle music played by Paddy Glackin

The Wandering Minstrel

(Robbie plays two duets with Paddy), Gael Linn Records 1991; 'The Drones and the Chanters' (vol. 2), Robbie plays three tracks on this 1995 recording for Claddagh Records; 'Séidean Sí (Fairy Wind)', Robbie teams up again with Paddy Glackin on this recording of fiddle and pipe duets, Gael Linn Records 1995.

CHAPTER SEVEN

On Stage

Traditional Irish music is, as we have seen, a very social activity. Players and listeners gather together in a relaxed atmosphere where everyone participates directly in the enjoyment of the music. There is, however, another face to traditional music, a more public face, when the music is presented on stage by musicians for fee-paying concert-goers. This is not a new phenomenon. Fiddlers Michael Coleman, Paddy Killoran and James Morrison often played in American concert halls in the 1920s and 1930s. At the turn of the century pipers such as Patsy Touhey performed in music halls in New York, Boston and Chicago.

Stage performance goes hand-in-hand with the recording industry. The musicians that recorded in America earlier this century were also the musicians that took to the stage.

It was not until the 1960s that traditional music began to be recorded and performed in concert halls and theatres in Ireland. The man responsible for the promotion of traditional Irish music at this time was Seán Ó Riada. He had played the fiddle as a child, therefore he was very familiar with traditional music. He combined this with his extensive knowledge of classical music and gathered together a 'folk

Seán Ó Riada

orchestra' which he called Ceoltóirí Cualann. They played arrangements of traditional tunes and old harp music as well as some of Ó Riada's own compositions. Ó Riada himself played the harpsichord with Ceoltóirí Cualann. This was an unusual accompaniment for pipes, fiddles, flutes, whistles and accordion and gave the group a very sophisticated sound. Some of the musicians in Ceoltóirí Cualann continued playing together as a group under the direction of piper Paddy Moloney. They have become the most well-known and widely-travelled of all traditional Irish groups, The Chieftains. Their line-up of instruments includes flute, pipes, whistle, fiddles, harp and bodhrán.

The early Chieftains

The Chieftains have recorded over twenty CDs and have played all over the world, including China. They have done more to popularise traditional Irish music than any other group and are still continuing to do so.

Many successful bands followed in the footsteps of The Chieftains. Planxty had a combination of instruments never used together before. Liam O'Flynn provided the melody on uillean pipes and was accompanied by bouzouki, mandolin,

Planxty

guitar and sometimes bodhrán. As well as dance tunes, they performed a lot of songs in their own innovative way. They had an instantly recognisable sound because of the instruments they played and the way they arranged the music and accompaniment.

The Bothy Band used guitar, bouzouki and clavinet to accompany tunes played on pipes, fiddle and flute. The clavinet is an electric keyboard that sounds a bit like a harpsichord and it gave the Bothy Band a very full, powerful sound. Donal Lunny, one of the founders of Planxty, also played bouzouki with the Bothy Band.

The bouzouki, this time played by Alec Finn, featured in another group based in Galway, Dé Danann. Their early recordings included Charlie Pigott on banjo, Frankie Gavin on fiddle, Johnny 'Ringo' McDonagh

The Bothy Band

on bodhran as well as Alec Finn. Dé Danann had a raw, energetic sound. Not all the tunes they played were traditional; they recorded a very interesting version of a well-known Beatles song, 'Hey Jude', and later experimented with various pieces by G.F. Handel and J.S. Bach. Their most recent CD includes a version of the rock group Queen's song 'Bohemian Rhapsody'.

Dé Danann

The most exciting group of recent years is Altan. Fronted by talented fiddler and singer Mairéad Ní Mhaonaigh, they have a huge repertoire of Donegal tunes. The group was started by Mairéad and her flute-playing husband Frankie Kennedy. Sadly Frankie died in 1994, but Mairéad was determined that Altan should

Altan

continue after all the time and effort he had put into their music. They have made some great recordings of traditional music , the most recent being 'Runaway Sunday'.

As we have seen, what we call traditional music has become 'Irish' over a long period of time. Influences were absorbed from other cultures. Other influences were rejected and over the centuries the essential 'Irishness' has emerged. Outside influences are still affecting traditional music. The use of African drums, didgeridoos and electric instruments is becoming more common. The Sharon Shannon Band, for example, use drums and bass to give the music a very modern

Sharon Shannon

feel. They play an interesting mix of traditional tunes and world music. Today there are more musicians such as East Clare fiddler Martin Hayes, and groups like Dervish, Solas, Lunasa and Lá Lugh playing on stages all over the world. The huge success of Riverdance has brought traditional Irish music to the ears of many people who would otherwise never have heard it. Thus the process of tradition continues and will continue, so that traditional music can be part of modern life in the twenty-first century.

Other books in the Exploring Series from THE O'BRIEN PRESS

EXPLORING THE BOOK OF KELLS

George Otto Simms

Reconstruction drawings: David Rooney
Full colour reproductions from the Book of Kells

A beautiful and simple introduction.

Joint winner with *Brendan the Navigator* of the Irish Children's Book Trust BOOK OF THE DECADE AWARD

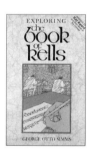

Hardback £6.95/$12.95

BRENDAN THE NAVIGATOR

George Otto Simms

Reconstruction drawings: David Rooney

'A perfect book ... As with his previous bestseller Simms has shone his craftsman's light of love on the world of Brendan and made it live.' RTE GUIDE

Paperback £4.50/$7.95

ST PATRICK

George Otto Simms

Reconstruction drawings: David Rooney

The real story of St Patrick, Ireland's patron saint.

'A new interpretation and explanation by a leading scholar' LEINSTER LEADER

'Charming and elegant account'
IRELAND OF THE WELCOMES

Paperback £4.95/$7.95

THE WORLD OF COLMCILLE

ALSO KNOWN AS COLUMBA
Mairéad Ashe FitzGerald

Reconstruction drawings: Stephen Hall

The life and times of this complex and powerful man who was a leading figure in the politics, religion and art of his day.

Hardback £8.99/$12.95

THE VIKINGS IN IRELAND

Morgan Llywelyn

Reconstruction drawings: David Rooney

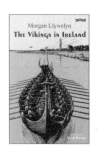

An exciting blend of fact and fiction by a master writer and storyteller, telling the colourful history of the Vikings ... and stirring the imagination.

Hardback £7.99/$12.95

THE CELTIC WAY OF LIFE

Curriculum Development Unit

Reconstruction drawings: Josip Lizatovic

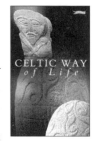

The lifestyle of the early pagan Celts explored – their home life, political organisation, hunting, fighting, work, leisure, art, building, celebrations, beliefs.

Paperback £5.99/$9.95

Send for our full colour catalogue
These books are available from your bookseller. In case of difficulty you may order direct, using this form.